AMAZING ART FORMS

The Art of Sculpting

BY MARLEY RICHMOND

Kids Core
An Imprint of Abdo Publishing
abdobooks.com

abdobooks.com

Printed in the United States of America, North Mankato, Minnesota.
102024
012025

THIS BOOK CONTAINS RECYCLED MATERIALS

Cover Photo: Shutterstock Images
Interior Photos: Shutterstock Images, 4–5, 10–11, 13, 26, 29 (bottom); Maria Symchych/Shutterstock Images, 7; Paolo Gallo/Shutterstock Images, 8; Gareth Cattermole/Getty Images Entertainment/Getty Images, 15 (top left); Chris Jackson/Chris Jackson Collection/Getty Images, 15 (top right), 15 (middle left); Ian Gavan/Getty Images Entertainment/Getty Images, 15 (middle right), 15 (bottom); Emily Marie Wilson/Shutterstock Images, 16; Hayk Shalunts/Shutterstock Images, 18–19; Adoc-Photos/Corbis Historical/Getty Images, 21; Sergi Reboredo/VW Pics/Universal Images Group/Getty Images, 22; Feng Wuyong/Xinhua/Imago/Alamy, 25; Natasha Breen/Shutterstock Images, 28 (top); Misa Lukic/Shutterstock Images, 28 (bottom); Nowra Photography/Shutterstock Images, 29 (top)

Editor: Haley Williams
Series Designer: Katharine Hale

Library of Congress Control Number: 2024938375

Publisher's Cataloging-in-Publication Data

Names: Richmond, Marley, author.
Title: The art of sculpting / by Marley Richmond
Description: Minneapolis, Minnesota: ABDO Publishing, 2025 | Series: Amazing art forms | Includes online resources and index.
Identifiers: ISBN 9781098295813 (lib. bdg.) | ISBN 9798384916819 (ebook)
Subjects: LCSH: Art--Juvenile literature. | Sculpture--Juvenile literature. | Stonework, Decorative--Juvenile literature. | Sculpture materials--Juvenile literature. | Sculptors--Juvenile literature. | Sculpture--Technique--Juvenile literature. | Arts and history--Juvenile literature.
Classification: DDC 730--dc23

CONTENTS

Artists may use a variety of tools, including their hands, when working with clay.

CHAPTER 1

Creating a Coil Pot

Aisha pulled a small ball of moist clay from a plastic bag. Aisha's art class was learning how to make coil pots. Coils are long ropes of clay. Aisha used two hands to roll her ball of clay back and forth on the table. It grew longer and thinner.

The clay started to dry out. Aisha sprayed it with water to keep it moist.

When Aisha had a long coil, she began wrapping it into a spiral. Aisha used a metal pin tool to score the clay. She scratched thin lines into the top and bottom of the coil. Then she added a little bit of watery clay, called slip, over the scored coil. As she wrapped the coil, she

Polymer Clay

Polymer clay is a good material for beginner artists. It does not require special equipment. Artists use their hands to warm up polymer clay. It becomes softer and easier to mold when it is warm. Once artists have created their clay sculptures, they bake them in an oven. This hardens the sculptures into their final product.

Keeping clay moist prevents it from cracking and makes it easier to work with.

pressed the scored sides together. This would help the clay stick together.

Aisha continued to wrap the coil around in circles. She used her fingers to smooth it out. Soon she had a small bowl! Once Aisha's bowl was dry, the teacher would bake it in a kiln. A kiln is a special oven for clay that heats to about 2,380 degrees Fahrenheit (1,300°C). Baking the bowl would make it strong. Aisha was excited to try creating a more detailed sculpture next time.

The stone statue *David* by Michelangelo is one of the most famous sculptures in art history.

What Is Sculpting?

Sculpture is a type of three-dimensional (3D) art. That means it is not flat. Many early sculptures were useful objects. People added decorations to everyday items such as bowls and vases. Other sculptures showed figures, including people and animals. A person who creates sculptures is called a sculptor.

Today, artists use many techniques and mediums when sculpting. A medium is a type of material used to create art. Some artists mold soft clay. Others carve hard stone. Artists sculpt to create beauty, honor subjects, and show emotions through art.

Further Evidence

Look at the website below. Does it give any new evidence to support Chapter One?

Sculpture

abdocorelibrary.com/art-of-sculpting

Some artists use pottery wheels to create sculptures. A pottery wheel spins in a circle as the artist shapes wet clay by hand or using tools.

CHAPTER 2

Techniques and Mediums

Each artist decides what medium and technique to use for a sculpture. An artist might think about the final size, location, and design of their artwork. Some mediums, such as stone or metal, are strong but heavy. They work well for outdoor sculptures.

Other mediums such as clay are easy to work with and require few tools.

Modeling and Carving

Modeling is a technique artists use to mold a material into shapes. Artists may use tools or their hands to create details. They may add or take away some material. This works best with soft mediums such as clay.

Moist clay is easy to mold. Artists allow finished sculptures to dry completely. Then sculptures are **fired** in a kiln. After clay is fired, it is hard and strong.

Carving is the process of removing material from a solid block. Artists often carve stone and wood. But this technique works with

People use a liquid called glaze to decorate their clay sculptures. Glaze comes in many colors.

many materials. First, artists cut away large chunks of material. This way they can find the basic shape of their piece. Then, they work on the details. Artists use tools such as hammers and **chisels** to carve stone. Knives and **gouges** are often used on wood.

Casting and Assembling

To cast a sculpture, artists pour liquid into a mold. The mold is in the shape of the final sculpture. Once the liquid hardens, it can be removed from the mold. This process is often used with metal or liquid clay. Many artists create their own molds for casting.

Kinetic Sculptures

Kinetic sculptures are artworks that move. Wind, flowing water, or magnets move some kinetic sculptures. Motors power others. Famous sculptor Alexander Calder created hanging kinetic sculptures. As air moves around the sculptures, they shift. This creates new patterns and shadows.

Casting Metal

Some artists use reusable molds to cast their metal sculptures. Others use molds that can be used only once.

STEP 1

Sculpt a pattern from soft material.

STEP 2

Press the pattern into a sand mixture.

STEP 3

Let the sand mixture harden into a mold.

STEP 4

Melt the metal and pour into the mold.

STEP 5

Remove the sculpture from the mold and polish.

Portuguese artist Bordalo II creates sculptures of animals that are made of trash and old items.

Assembled sculptures are created when artists put materials together to form a single piece. Sculptors can use different mediums for this technique. They may bend, twist, and **weld** metal objects. Or they may cut and glue pieces of wood. Some artists use several types of mediums for one sculpture.

Explore Online

Visit the website below. Does it give any new information about how to carve sculptures?

Soap Carving

abdocorelibrary.com/art-of-sculpting

Jeff Koons was an artist who made colorful sculptures that look like everyday objects. *Balloon Dog* is one of his most famous works.

CHAPTER 3

Sculptors and Museums

Throughout history, many sculptors have become famous for their work. Some artists create sculptures that are taller than skyscrapers. Others make sculptures that are small enough for a person to hold.

Famous Sculptors

Michelangelo was an Italian artist. He lived during a period known as the Renaissance. Michelangelo worked from the late 1400s to the mid-1500s. He is well-known for his marble sculptures. *David* is one of his most famous works.

Auguste Rodin was a French sculptor. He worked from the mid-1800s to the early 1900s. His sculptures are realistic. They include many textures and details on their surfaces. One of his most famous sculptures is *The Thinker*. It shows an artist thinking deeply. Several versions of the sculpture can be found around the world.

Ana Mendieta's sculptures represent her identity as a Cuban American woman.

August Rodin is known as the father of modern sculpture because he broke away from traditional sculpting techniques.

She created her Silueta series between 1973 and 1980. Each artwork shows the **imprint** of her body. Mendieta makes these imprints in different natural areas. These include a grassy field and a sandy beach.

Louise Bourgeois's spider sculptures can be found in countries around the world, including Spain, Japan, and the United States.

Louise Bourgeois created installation sculptures. These are large sculptures that are designed for a specific place. Bourgeois lived from 1911 to 2010. Some of her most famous works are sculptures of large metal spiders. The spiders stand for the negative memories from Bourgeois's childhood. But their webs represent healing.

Roberto Lugo is a clay sculptor. He was born in 1981. Lugo makes pots that combine traditional designs with modern culture. He uses sculpture to start conversations about social issues such as **racism**.

Sculpture Gardens

Many sculptures are in museums. But some are too large to go inside buildings. Sculpture gardens are outdoor spaces where people can see large sculptures.

Ekebergparken is in Oslo, Norway. Visitors can find many sculptures there. One is called *The Dance*. It is by George Cutts. Two metal rods twist around in this kinetic sculpture. The park also displays a huge, colorful sculpture by Niki de Saint Phalle.

Hakone Open-Air Museum is in Hakone, Japan. This park includes many sculptures

The Statue of Liberty

The Statue of Liberty is a huge statue in New York City. The sculpture stands 305 feet (93 m) tall. It was designed by French sculptor Frédéric-Auguste Bartholdi in the late 1800s. The Statue of Liberty is made of thin copper. This is a light material. A steel structure inside the statue supports it.

Woods of Net by Toshiko Horiuchi MacAdam is an interactive sculpture that was made for children to climb and play on.

by Henry Moore. He created sculptures of **abstract** human figures. Visitors can also see *Floating Sculpture 3* by Marta Pan. This large red sculpture floats in a pond. It moves with the wind.

Spoonbridge and Cherry is a well-known fountain by Claes Oldenburg and Coosje van Bruggen. It is found in the Minneapolis Sculpture Garden.

The Minneapolis Sculpture Garden is in Minnesota. Visitors can walk through the sculpture *Okciyapi*. It was created by American Indian artist Angela Two Stars. The sculpture invites people to sit together. They can learn about the Dakota American Indian language.

Not all sculptures are found in museums and sculpture parks. People around the world make interesting sculptures every day. Sculpting is an exciting art form for anyone to try.

Primary Source

Sculptor Roberto Lugo talks about how making clay sculptures allows him to express himself and his experiences. He says:

> [Pottery] gives me an opportunity to take all those things . . . that happened to me . . . and make something out of it. Make something out of myself.

Source: "Roberto Lugo, NCECA Emerging Artist." *YouTube*, uploaded by WatchNCECA, 30 Mar. 2015, youtube.com. Accessed 8 Apr. 2024.

Point of View

What is the author's point of view on this topic? What is your point of view? Write a short essay about how they are similar and different.

Art Supplies

Clay and sculpting tools

Stone, chisel, and hammer

Wood and gouges

Metal and welding equipment

Glossary

abstract
general shapes and colors that achieve an effect rather than realistically representing a subject

chisels
sharp metal tools used to carve or chip solid materials

fired
heated to make stronger

gouges
rounded chisels used to scoop away solid material

imprint
a mark made by pressing something hard into something soft

racism
the belief that a person or group of people is lesser than another because of race or ethnicity

weld
to join two pieces of metal by melting them together

Online Resources

To learn more about sculpting, visit our free resource websites below.

Core Library CONNECTION
FREE! COMMON CORE MULTIMEDIA RESOURCES

Visit **abdocorelibrary.com** or scan this QR code for free Common Core resources for teachers and students, including vetted activities, multimedia, and booklinks, for deeper subject comprehension.

Booklinks NONFICTION NETWORK
FREE! ONLINE NONFICTION RESOURCES

Visit **abdobooklinks.com** or scan this QR code for free additional online weblinks for further learning. These links are routinely monitored and updated to provide the most current information available.

Learn More

Anderson, Kirsten. *Who Was Michelangelo?* Penguin Workshop, 2022.

Peterson, Tamara J. M., and Ruthie Van Oosbree. *Sculpt It!: Super Simple Crafts for Kids.* Abdo, 2023.

Index

About the Author

Marley Richmond is a children's book editor and author. She lives in Minnesota with her cat, Bean. Marley and her mom share a clay studio and enjoy making art together.